AN IRISH WHISTLE TUNE BOOK

Suitable for Fiddle, Flute, Pipes, Concertina, Accordion, Mandolin, etc.
by
Tom Maguire

OSSIAN

For a catalogue of all our publications and distributed items of
Irish and other music please send your name and address to:
OSSIAN PUBLICATIONS
14-15 Berners Street, London W1T 3LJ, UK.

Published by
OSSIAN PUBLICATIONS

Exclusive distributors:
Hal Leonard,
7777 West Bluemound Road,
Milwaukee, WI 53213
Email: info@halleonard.com

Hal Leonard Europe Limited,
42 Wigmore Street Maryleborne,
London, WIU 2 RY
Email: info@halleonardeurope.com

Hal Leonard Australia Pty. Ltd.
4 Lentara Court Cheltenham,
Victoria, 9132 Australia
Email: info@halleonard.com.au

OMB106
ISBN 978-0-94600-591-8

Design and layout by John Loesberg.
Special thanks to Geraldine Cotter, Tomás O Cannain, Matt Cranitch,
'Hammy' Hamilton, Tom Stephens and the Tradional Music Archive,
Dublin.

Cover Picture: St. Patrick's Close, by Walter Osbourne (1859-1903)
reproduced by permission of The National Gallery of Ireland.`

Printed in the EU.

www.halleonard.com

CONTENTS

From every twilit archway
The shawly girls would slip,
And link their boys beneath it,
And flutes would lead a step

from: A Statue to Life
Frank O'Connor

STILL I LOVE HIM

IM BIM BABARO

THE STAR OF THE COUNTY DOWN

Cuaichín Ó

The Poor Irish Boy

Ar Éirinn Ní Neosfainn Cé Hí

CARRICKFERGUS

A Bunch of Thyme

Pilib an Cheoil

THE DERRY AIR

Thugamar Féin an Samhradh Linn

AN CHÚILFHIONN

BLIND MARY

THE BANTRY GIRLS' LAMENT

An Cailín Deas Rua

THE CLIFFS OF DOONEEN

COME BACK PADDY REILLY

Siobhán Ní Dhuibhir

Lord Inchiquin

Carolan

THE THREE SEA CAPTAINS

THE LONG NOTE

SARATOGA HORNPIPE

THE VERSEVIENNA

24

Oíche Nollaig

PLANXTY IRWIN

Carolan

AN BUACHAILL CAOL DUBH

Sweeney's Dream

The Blacksmith's Reel

SWEENEY'S POLKA

THE BALLYDESMOND POLKA

WHELAN'S JIG

MUNSTER BUTTERMILK

DONEGAL MAZURKA

Sonny's Mazurka

THE OLD SHADY BOHEREEN

GOING TO THE WELL FOR WATER

KATHLEEN HEHIR

THE BOY IN THE GAP

THE BOY IN THE BOAT

A Wet December

THE BAG OF SPUDS

ANDERSONS